A SIMPLE GUIDE TO PRAYER

A SIMPLE GUIDE TO PRAYER

Jack Hay

RITCHIE

John Ritchie Publishing

40 Beansburn, Kilmarnock, Scotland

ISBN-13: 978 1 914273 09 4

Copyright © 2021 by John Ritchie Ltd.
40 Beansburn, Kilmarnock, Scotland

www.ritchiechristianmedia.co.uk

Typeset by John Ritchie Ltd., Kilmarnock
Printed by Bell & Bain Ltd., Glasgow

Contents

Chapter 1

A SIMPLE GUIDE?

Perhaps the title of this booklet is a little misleading since it uses the word "simple" in connection with prayer! There is a simplicity about prayer, because basically, it is just speaking to God, but there is a complexity about it as well. For example, the Bible tells us that "we know not what we should pray for as we ought" (Rom 8.26), indicating that there are circumstances in which we are at a loss to know how best to frame our requests. Like ourselves, the disciples were aware of being out of their depth and, on one occasion when the Lord had finished praying, one of them said, "Teach us to pray" (Lk 11.1). In the subsequent verses in what is commonly called The Lord's Prayer, the Saviour outlined a framework that gives guidance about how to structure our prayers. He followed that by telling a parable and then giving teaching that would encourage us to be bold, persistent and expectant when we do speak to our Father. The point is though, the request of that disciple shows that **we need to be taught to pray**.

A previous publication gave simple guidance for Bible study, and to complement that, this is an attempt to cover some of the Bible's teaching about prayer. We will base this on **the Bible's teaching,** and will deliberately avoid anecdotes from modern life such as remarkable answers to prayers that have been recorded in some interesting contemporary biographies. Doubtless, incorporating some of these stories would lighten the reading for you, but instead, I will just appeal to you to hang in there!

In the Christian life, Bible reading and prayer are inseparable, for time spent alone in fellowship with God is a strong foundation for our spiritual lives. His Word is the means by which He communicates to us, and even as we read we can respond to Him in prayer as He provides encouragement, or issues a command, or gives an exhortation. Sometimes what we read makes an impression, or brings conviction to our hearts that makes us want to respond, and so we speak to our Father. As we read, He speaks to us, and as we pray, we speak to Him and thus the link of communion is forged.

Undoubtedly, there is something puzzling about prayer. We know from the Word that we are petitioning a God Who "worketh all things after the counsel of his own will" (Eph 1.11), and so we refer to Him as being sovereign. "Who hath been his counsellor?" (Rom 11.34). He does not need advisors, He cannot be influenced, and His purpose is fixed. Does that mean that if what He has decreed is rigid, it is pointless to appeal to Him? No, that would be a false perception.

Scripture does tell us that "The effectual fervent prayer of a righteous man availeth much" (Jas 5.16), and Elijah is cited as an example of that. So the Word of God encourages us to see great value in prayer: and to believe that God does answer prayer; "Call unto me, and I will answer thee, and shew thee great and mighty things, which thou knowest not" (Jer 33.3). I repeat; there is something unfathomable about that, but it seems to indicate that God's sovereign decrees factor in the prayers of His believing people, and thus there is the invitation to "come boldly unto the throne of grace" (Heb 4.16). In fact, it is not merely an invitation; it is a summons, a command in Scripture: "Pray without ceasing" (1 Thess 5.17). Are we obeying that command?

Be sure about this, prayer does help: "Ye also **helping together by prayer for us**" (2 Cor 1.11). "This shall turn to my salvation **through your prayer**, and the supply of the Spirit of Jesus Christ" (Phil 1:19). Paul believed that while God was superintending his circumstances, the prayers of His people were a considerable factor in each new development. An old saying is that "prayer moves the hand that moves the universe". Or again, "prayer is the slender nerve that moves the muscles of omnipotence". So then, while we may not understand the relationship between God's firm intentions and our earnest pleas, the Scriptures never suggest that we should be preoccupied with that enigma. What should challenge us is this; there are multiple Bible passages in which the **command** to pray is unmistakeable and uncompromising. So whether we understand the complexities of prayer or not, we are under obligation to pray.

James Montgomery wrote a delightful hymn about prayer, but two lines will be sufficient here.

> *Prayer is the Christian's vital breath,*
> *The Christian's native air.*

The poet was inferring that, for the believer, praying should be as natural as breathing, and that we ought to be living in the very atmosphere of prayer. J.C. Ryle wrote that "prayer is to faith what breath is to life". It is illustrated in the conversion story of Saul of Tarsus, the Apostle Paul. No sooner was he saved, than it was said of him, "Behold, he prayeth" (Acts 9.11). This seemed to be the spontaneous outcome of having been born again; the new child in the family of God was now speaking to his Father.

Having said that, most of us would acknowledge that the time that we spend in prayer is often limited, our commitment to it is half-hearted, and it is only in an emergency that we become really earnest and persistent in praying. We may hear regular sermons and read various books on the topic of prayer and yet somehow, we are all aware that a deficient prayer-life is far too common. So, as this little publication goes out, if it can help just a few of you to develop a scripturally-motivated and scripturally-based prayer life, then it will have hit the target.

Chapter 2

HOW PRAYER BEGAN

The First Prayers

What Adam and Cain said to God could hardly be described as prayer! In fact, when God took issue with them, they were both rather insolent in their responses. A general statement is made about the first prayers in Genesis 4.26 when Adam's grandson Enos was born: "Then began men to call upon the name of the Lord". The baby's name means '*frail mortal man*', so it was **when** men began to realise just how frail and vulnerable they were, **then** they began to look heavenward and ask for assistance. This incident at the dawn of history teaches us that prayer is an acknowledgement of our own weakness and an admission of our dependence on God.

This is a crucial lesson. Do you feel self-reliant, able to cope, impregnable, resourceful? If we seldom pray we are unconsciously declaring that we are all of these things! We are almost replicating the attitude of unbelievers who declare proudly, "I don't need a crutch!" Prayer is one way of expressing our total reliance upon God.

We are told frequently about David that he "enquired of the Lord" (e.g. 2 Sam 5.19; 23). Although he was a skilled soldier, he felt the need to ask for divine guidance and divine support. There were two occasions in Joshua's life when he failed to consult God and acted on his own initiative. The first was at Ai, and then when the subtle Gibeonites tried to deceive him, and on both occasions it ended in disaster (Josh 7.2-4; 9.3-27). In the second incident, Scripture says specifically, that he "asked not counsel at the mouth of the Lord" (v 14). These stand as a stark warning to us. It will always end in tears when we make decisions and press ahead without praying, or when we react quickly to circumstances without referring the crisis to God first. Inevitably we saddle ourselves with difficulties. "Commit thy way unto the Lord; trust also in him; and he shall bring it to pass" (Ps 37.5).

Abraham, Isaac and Jacob

Genesis records some accounts of men praying to God, although the word prayer is not often used. Regularly, we read of Abraham calling on the name of the Lord. He is perceived as the great man of faith and, apart from a few lapses, he lived his life in dependence on God; faith and dependence are almost synonymous terms. His attitude underscores the lesson from Genesis 4.

Isaac too "called upon the name of the Lord" (Gen 26.25). It is evident that his father's influence had been felt, and Abraham's attitude of dependence was being duplicated in the life of his son. This teaches us that it is worth being a prayer warrior from the viewpoint of setting an example to others, particularly to our children. Hannah was a praying mother (1 Sam 1-2), and in the few years that she had her son Samuel she must have shown him by example the importance of praying for the people; thus "Samuel cried unto the Lord for Israel; and the Lord heard him" (ch. 7.9). He was so convinced of the importance of prayer that he would have regarded it as sinful had he neglected to pray for them: "God forbid that I should sin against the Lord in ceasing to pray for you" (ch.12.23). As a very young child, he had learned from his mother just how vital prayer is. Without being showy or appearing super-spiritual, let your commitment to the life of prayer encourage your family and friends to see its value for themselves.

Jacob had a history of relying on his own resourcefulness, and attempting to manipulate things for his own advantage, but when he heard of his brother approaching with 400 men in tow, he assumed that Esau was intent on fulfilling his intention to kill him. This time, there was no hiding place (Gen 32) and his fear drove him into the presence of God. He expressed his perplexity that this calamity should have overtaken him when he was following divine instructions (v 9), he acknowledged his unworthiness (v 10), and he called on God to help him in accordance with His promise (vv 11-12). The crisis had brought him to the limit of his own resources, and caused him to feel the need of help from heaven. We should not need an emergency to force us to turn to God, but, at the same time, it is good to know that He is available for us when we do face a predicament. So, there are these lessons to be learned from the lives of the patriarchs in early days, at a time when men were beginning to understand that "the eyes of the Lord are over the righteous, and his ears are open unto their prayers: but the face of the Lord is against them that do evil" (1 Pet 3.12).

Slaves in Egypt

In the early chapters of Exodus, we are introduced to a nation of slaves trapped in the land of Egypt. What God said to Moses at the burning bush (Ex 3.7-8) illustrates the truth of the verse just quoted from 1 Peter. "I have surely **seen** the affliction of my people which are in Egypt"; His eyes. "I have **heard** their cry"; His ears. "I am come down to deliver them **out of the hand of the Egyptians**"; His face against the evildoers. We are learning that God's whole being is devoted to the welfare of His people. His ears are attentive to agonising cries for help.

Psalm 121.1 is likely best understood as being two questions. "Shall I lift up mine eyes unto the hills?" - the places where the heathen had their idols. Never! "From whence cometh **my** help?" and the answer is supplied in v 2, "My help cometh from the Lord, which made heaven and earth", this divine Helper who neither slumbers not sleeps (vv 3-4). The Psalmist had already proved His faithfulness, for in the previous psalm he had said, "In my distress I cried unto the Lord, and he helped me" (Ps 120.1). He had learned the lesson that his forefathers had discovered at the Exodus, that in our distress, God hears anguished prayers, and is superlatively equipped to move to meet the need. The fact that He is "the Lord who made heaven and earth" indicates that His power is limitless, and there is nothing too hard for Him (Gen 18.14). John Newton of *Amazing Grace* fame also wrote this:

> *Thou art coming to a King;*
> *Large petitions with thee bring;*
> *For His grace and power are such,*
> *None can ever ask too much.*

So from these early books of the Bible, the lesson is plain; we are dependent on God, He hears our prayers, and He has the power to meet our needs.

Chapter 3

PRAY WITHOUT CEASING

"Pray without ceasing" is one of the shortest verses in the Bible (1 Thess 5.17). Despite its brevity, it is extremely pointed and relevant. It obviously does not infer that the brothers who participate in a prayer meeting should monopolise the time! Nor does it suggest that we have to be on our knees for hour after hour in our personal devotions. It is obviously an encouragement to be regular and persistent in prayer. When Paul brought his teaching about the "whole armour of God" to a climax, he highlighted the fact that persistent prayer contributes to our spiritual protection: "praying **always** with all prayer and supplication in the Spirit" (Eph 6.17-18). The word "always" denotes the need to be consistent and resolute.

The Lord Jesus told a parable to reinforce the point: "Men ought always to pray, and not to faint" (Lk 18.1-8). The widow in the story harassed the unjust judge. He spoke of "her continual coming" and of the fact that she troubled him and was likely to weary him. The judge cannot illustrate God, depicting Him as a God Who is reluctant to respond to our prayers unless we wear Him down! No; the point of the parable is that we should be as tenacious as the widow, illustrated again from the life of Jacob when he said to the Divine Wrestler, "I will not let thee go, except thou bless me" (Gen 32.26).

There are two Old Testament characters whose prayer lives were exemplary and instructive, and who in different ways illustrate the "pray without ceasing" command. The first is Daniel, and the other is Nehemiah.

Daniel

Daniel prayed without ceasing in the sense that "he kneeled upon his knees **three times a day**, and prayed, and gave thanks before his God" (Dan 6.10). This was in a time of crisis when prayer had been outlawed, but because it had been the habit of his life, he still did it, "as he did aforetime". While there are many lessons from the passage, the main emphasis is on the fact that this was something that he did methodically and regularly. David had the same routine. "Evening, and morning, and at noon, will I pray, and cry aloud" (Ps 55.17). A pattern of precise, disciplined appointments with God should be reproduced in each of our lives. If we establish the healthy habit of praying at regular times each day, it will go a long way to holding to the principle of praying without ceasing. It is true that habits can become stale, but it is far better to be disciplined than to treat something as important as prayer haphazardly, an exercise that gets pushed to the side should something "more important" turn up. Daniel's enemies could set their clock by his approach into the presence of God!

Nehemiah

Very likely Nehemiah's prayer life was as well-ordered as Daniel's (Neh 1.4-11), but there was another dimension to it that illustrates a different aspect of praying without ceasing. As he lived his life, and as daily events unfolded, just where he was at any time, he lifted his heart to God in prayer. For example, when King Artaxerxes asked him about the reason for his sad face and then enquired about how he could assist, in a split second Nehemiah "prayed to the God of heaven" and then responded to the king (ch. 2.1-5). Later, when he was ridiculed by the Samaritans, he immediately turned to God: "Hear, O our God; for we are despised" (ch. 4.4). In the process of sorting out problems among the Jewish leaders, again he just looked heavenward for help, "Remember me, O my God, concerning this" (ch. 13.14). Each of these impromptu prayers was brief, pointed and earnest, and they demonstrate that in every circumstance we can fire off a spontaneous prayer, and in that sense we can pray without ceasing.

If something comes in to your mind that you feel you should pray about, there is no need to save it till the close of the day. Just at the moment, and just where you are, the sharp short petition can be sent heavenward. So pray without ceasing in the sense of having your regular meetings with God in private, but pray without ceasing in the sense of living in the atmosphere of prayer, where at any moment you can refer matters to your Father in heaven.

Chapter 4

THE CONTENT OF OUR PRAYERS

Structure

Jude speaks about "praying in the Holy Spirit" (v 20), which conveys the idea that when we are praying, the Holy Spirit can lead us along from one matter to the next. As in Christian living and Christian service, He is our guide. So it is perhaps inappropriate to use the word "structure" in connection with our prayers, as if every prayer had to follow some prescribed formula. Having said that, when the Lord Jesus was teaching about prayer, He did say, "After this manner therefore pray ye" (Mt 6.9). What is generally called "The Lord's Prayer" was not given to be recited congregationally as part of a liturgy, but as guidance for our personal prayers. So there are general principles to be observed in the way the Lord arranged it.

It commences with an element of worship, as appreciation is expressed for the holiness of God's character. The Lord did teach us to address God as "Father", reminding us of His tenderness, affection, and interest, but He also encouraged us to keep His holiness in mind. In other words, the sense of privilege at being in a warm relationship with God should never diminish our reverence for Him Who is "the high and lofty One that inhabiteth eternity, whose name is Holy" (Is 57.15).

Another fact that emerges here is that prayer should be addressed to God the Father. Later the Lord Jesus taught that we should address our prayers to the Father in His name: "that whatsoever ye shall ask of the Father in my name, he may give it you" (Jn 15.16). "In that day ye shall ask me nothing. Verily, verily, I say unto you, Whatsoever ye shall ask the Father in my name, he will give it you" (Jn 16.23. See also v 26). If you examine prayers in the epistles, you will see the outworking of the Lord's teaching, and the ratification of His instructions. For example, "giving thanks to God the Father through him" (Col 3.17 RV). The vast majority of New Testament prayers were addressed to the Father.

Note too that in the Lord's Prayer God's interests take priority: His kingdom and His will. Too often, our prayers are just a list of our own wants. Having said that, our own basic needs can be expressed, such as the necessity for our daily bread. The mention of sin as a debt involves confession, and an appeal for spiritual preservation is incorporated. There is a blend of differing sentiments, and in greater and lesser degrees, these can be the framework of our prayers, and feature in each of them. That leads us to consider some different aspects of prayer that can be incorporated in our devotions, features that we could call some of the ingredients of our prayers.

Confession

As well as the general word for prayer, the New Testament uses different words to describe various aspects of prayer, and these should all feature in our prayers. It may be well to start with confession, because it is only when there is a clear sky between God and ourselves that we can comfortably move on in our prayers.

In his first epistle, John gives comprehensive teaching about sin in the life of a believer. He shows quite clearly that if sin is still dominant in a person's life they could hardly regard themselves as being born again, for those who have been born again do not habitually practise sin (ch. 3.9). Having said that, he indicates that anyone who claims to be sinlessly perfect is self-deceived and untruthful (ch. 1.8,10). The bottom line is that there are times when Christians sin. When that takes place, the Lord Jesus immediately acts as our "advocate with the Father", with the aim of restoring the enjoyment of our relationship with the Father that sin has disturbed (ch. 2.1-2). For our part, the Father expects us to "confess our sins", and if that is undertaken, He is "faithful and just to forgive us our sins" (ch. 1.8-10). It is not that our sins have deprived us of our salvation, and that we need the kind of forgiveness that we received at conversion, but rather, this is a Father forgiving His child, so that the obstacle to enjoying His company has been removed. I would call this, family forgiveness.

It is important to incorporate any necessary confession in the early stages of your prayers, so that you can proceed without any sense of guilt and shame. Then you will know that the offending issue has been dealt with in a "faithful and just" way, because of the precious blood of Christ.

Supplication

The word "supplication" conveys the idea of praying earnestly about specific needs. Our prayers can be too general at times, so that it would be hard to know whether these prayers have been answered or not! They are too vague.

Some Bible supplications were expressed in dramatic circumstances, perhaps more dramatic than we will ever face. For example, when over a million Ethiopians attacked King Asa, his appeal was very definite, "Help us, O Lord our God; for we rest on thee, and in thy name we go against this multitude" (2 Chr 14.11). In similar circumstances, his son Jehoshaphat was equally pointed in his request: "O our God, wilt thou not judge them? for we have no might against this great company that cometh against us; neither know we what to do: but our eyes are upon thee" (ch 20.12). We may never face such overwhelming circumstances, but every new situation brings new challenges, with the need for fresh guidance, so we need to be very specific when bringing every matter to the Lord in prayer.

Intercession

Basically, intercession is praying for other people. Of course we pray about our own personal needs, but we dare not be self-centred in the way we approach God. It is not all about me, and my, and mine! It is an honour to speak to God about the needs of others. Remember Abraham's prayer of intercession when he pleaded with God for the people of Sodom. He regarded himself as being so insignificant, only "dust and ashes", and yet he took it upon himself to speak to the Lord as an intercessor (Gen 18.27).

It is in Luke's Gospel that the Lord Jesus is portrayed as the perfect man of prayer, but we know little of what He actually said. However, in John 17 there is a detailed account of one of His prayers, and for the more part, it is intercession. Eight verses are taken up with His own experience, but then a further eighteen are for His immediate disciples, and then for those who in course of time would believe on Him through their testimony. So a remarkable proportion of the prayer is devoted to intercession.

For whom can we pray? Paul prayed for **sinners**, people of his own nation who needed to be saved (Rom 10.1). We can pray for **servants**, the Lord's servants who are carrying the message of life to the needy. "Pray for us, that the word of the Lord may have free course, and be glorified" (2 Thess 3.1). The **saints** should have a big place in our prayers, and in fact, the majority of New Testament prayers were in the interests of believers, and in particular for their spiritual progress. Paul's epistles are permeated with prayer for his readers, for example, his prayer for the Colossians that they would "walk worthy of the Lord unto all pleasing" (Col 1.10). If you detect signs of spiritual deterioration in a fellow-believer, be quick to pray. When Peter was in grave spiritual danger, the Lord prayed specifically and personally for him; "I have prayed **for thee**" (Lk 22.32). We can pray for **the sick**. Perhaps the context of James 5 is special, but in the passage there is a general principle that those who are unwell can have a place in our prayers. In fact, John prayed particularly for his friend Gaius that he would be in health; John was in no doubt about his spiritual health, but he was praying that the man's physical health would match his spiritual prosperity (3 Jn 2). Intercessions should take in **the state** and its officials (1 Tim 2.1-2). Administrators at every level are in much need of divine wisdom and guidance.

It might be worth pointing out that in praying specifically and in interceding, there are some situations that are best kept for private prayer. Some believers may be uncomfortable about their personal circumstances being mentioned in a public prayer meeting, even although the intercessor is praying sincerely and earnestly. Someone sitting by could be a little embarrassed if you tell the Father in front of everyone else just how depressed they have become, or how a new set of circumstances has left them short of cash! These exaggerated examples are just to reinforce the appeal for tact when praying publicly.

Thanksgivings

When the Saviour healed the ten lepers, it grieved Him that only one of them returned to glorify God and express thanks: "Where are the nine?" (Lk 17.11-19). Of the heathen Paul said, "neither were (they) thankful" (Rom 1.21). A feature of the last days is that people are "unthankful" (2 Tim 3.2). The Scriptures teach that believers should always be thankful, and express that gratitude in their prayers. Private prayer should be full of thanksgiving, even when we are in circumstances that are making us anxious: "Be careful (anxious) for nothing; but in every thing by prayer and supplication **with thanksgiving** let your requests be made known unto God" (Phil 4.6). The same should be true of public prayers; when referring to the assembly prayer meeting, Paul speaks of "supplications, prayers, intercessions, **and giving of thanks**" (1 Tim 2.1). This theme will be developed in the next chapter.

Chapter 5

GRATITUDE

- It is God's will that you should be thankful (1 Thess 5.18).
- It is one of the evidences of being filled with the Spirit (Eph 5.20).
- It is commanded in Scripture: "and be ye thankful" (Col 3.15).
- It is regarded as "a sacrifice of praise" that pleases God (Heb 13.15-16).
- It is an echo of the song that is on the lips of angels, resounding through the heavens, as they "give glory and honour **and thanks** to him that sat on the throne" (Rev 4.9).

Taken together, these facts demonstrate that God places great value on expressions of gratitude in our prayers.

Does the Bible give guidance about suitable matters for thanksgiving? There are general statements in verses that have been alluded to that tell us, "In every thing give thanks" (1 Thess 5.18), or "giving thanks always for all things" (Eph 5.20).

These statements are very demanding, because they are really saying that whatever the situation we are in, we should be looking for something positive for which we can thank God. Jeremiah was sitting in a once bustling but now deserted city, a city ravaged by invasion and famine. In a situation like that he acknowledged that God's mercies were "new every morning", and that His faithfulness was great (Lam 3.22-23). Habakkuk resolved to "rejoice in the Lord" even when the fig tree would fail to blossom, and the vines, olive trees, fields and livestock would all produce a meagre yield (Hab 3.17-18). Despite their extremely fraught circumstances, these men found something for which they could praise God. Let us catch something of their disposition, rather than being like the ancient Israelites whose murmuring so angered God.

To be more specific, there are numerous Bible passages which provide us with material for thanksgiving. Anna arrived at the temple just when the Lord Jesus was being presented to the Lord, "and she coming in that instant gave thanks likewise unto the Lord" (Lk 2.38). She was going to speak about Him, but before she did so, she gave thanks for Him. There is an important lesson there. We should never be slow to speak about the Saviour, but our testimony will be warmer and more effective if we have spent time appreciating Him and giving thanks to the Father for Him first. Great fields of meditation open up to us when we reflect on the Lord Jesus, and everything about His Person and work stirs the heart with adoration. "Thanks be unto God for his unspeakable gift" (2 Cor 9.15). So we can give thanks for the **Saviour**.

Our **Salvation** is another cause for thankfulness. "God be thanked" (Rom 6.17-18); we had been the servants of sin, but are now free, the servants of righteousness. What a transformation! And Paul also felt "bound to give thanks always to God" for that future aspect of salvation which will result in "the obtaining of the glory of our Lord Jesus Christ" (2 Thess 2.13-14). It is often said that it is good to be saved; it is so good that we should never cease thanking God for it. Thank Him every day that you are bound for heaven and not hell.

We can also give thanks for the **Saints**, for there is so much about them that is worthy of praise to God. Paul introduced a number of his epistles by giving thanks for his readers, as he remembered his contact with them, their salvation and subsequent spiritual progress.

He thanked God for Christians at Rome whom he had never met, but the widespread news of their faith stirred him to praise God (Rom 1.8). Despite the range of problems at Corinth, he thanked God that the saints there had been graciously endowed with spiritual gifts (1 Cor 1.4-7). The faith and the impartial love of the Ephesians gave him cause for thanksgiving (Eph 1.15-16). The sacrificial giving of the Philippians to support him in the Lord's work touched him, and produced thanksgiving (Phil 1.3-5). Although he had never been to Colosse, the news of their faith and love moved him to thank God for the success of Gospel work there (Col 1.3-8). He thanked God for the earnest unrelenting labours of the Thessalonians (1 Thess 1.2-3). With the exception of the churches of Galatia, Paul found something for which to thank God in each of these assemblies to which he wrote.

Surely there is a lesson for us. We should be looking for something in every saint for which we can give thanks. Paul deeply appreciated Christian fellowship, for when a delegation from Rome met him on the last stages of his journey to the city, "he thanked God, and took courage" (Acts 28.15). Let us thank God regularly for the fellowship and support of the Lord's people.

Paul also gave God thanks for his **Service**, the fact that Christ had given him a ministry (1 Tim 1.12). That is something for which we can all be thankful, for it is a great honour to serve the living and true God. Is it not wonderful to think that God has not only saved us, but has given us opportunity to be engaged in reward-earning service for Him? He has given us the privilege in a hostile environment of being "ambassadors for Christ" (2 Cor 5.20), His representatives in a world that rejected Him and is still opposed to Him. The privilege should cause us to worship Him. He has not only given us the work, but He supplies us with all the spiritual and material resources we need to carry it through.

Another obvious cause for thanksgiving is the **Sustenance** that we enjoy daily. Having prayed for our daily bread, it is important to thank God for it. At the feeding of the 5000 and the feeding of the 4000 there is the record of the Lord giving thanks for the provision. In fact, it seems to be such an important highlight of the event that even when John was recalling it, he spoke of "the place where they did eat bread, **after that the Lord had given thanks**" (Jn 6.23). Mentioning the giving of thanks was not essential to the story-line, but it is recorded to demonstrate its importance. Interestingly, it was in a public place that the Lord gave thanks for the food, just a reminder that even in the environment of a café, restaurant or hotel dining room, it is appropriate to thank God for what has been provided. Paul even did it on the deck of a ship that was being battered by a gale! (Acts 27.35). God has created food for us, to "be received with thanksgiving" (1 Tim 4.3).

In the Psalms, time and again the poet finds a whole range of suitable material for thanksgiving. One quotation will be sufficient to demonstrate just how important gratitude is: "Bless the Lord, O my soul: and all that is within me, bless his holy name. Bless the Lord, O my soul, and forget not all his benefits" (Ps 103.1-2). So then, as far as our prayers are concerned, let there be that blend of supplication, intercession and giving of thanks.

Chapter 6

POSTURE AND PLACE

Posture; Kneeling

Sometimes the things that we sing express our aspirations rather than our actual experience! For example, one of Fanny Crosby's well-loved hymns is "I am Thine, O Lord". One of the verses is as follows:

> *O the pure delight of a single hour*
> *That before Thy throne I spend!*
> ***When I kneel in prayer***, *and with Thee, my God,*
> *I commune as friend with friend.*

We sing it so enthusiastically, but I wonder when last any of us did spend 'a single hour' kneeling in prayer, and finding it 'pure delight'? Does one hour seem too much? Time given to God in prayer is never wasted time; the more we pray, the healthier our spiritual lives will be.

The hymn speaks about kneeling in prayer, so is it necessary to kneel to pray? We are going to discover that it is not absolutely necessary, and, obviously, for some it would be a physical impossibility. The Bible describes a variety of postures for prayer, but it is clear from Scripture that both Old Testament and New Testament saints did kneel. At the inauguration of the temple, Solomon "kneeled down upon his knees before all the congregation of Israel" (2 Chr 6.13). Daniel has been cited already: "he kneeled upon his knees three times a day" (Dan 6.10). In private prayer, Paul bowed his knees "unto the Father of our Lord Jesus Christ" (Eph 3.14). When the elders from Ephesus were bidding him farewell, "he kneeled down, and prayed with them all" (Acts 20.36). The same happened at Tyre when he embarked on the last short leg of his sea journey: "we kneeled down on the shore, and prayed" (Acts 21.5). It appears that it was customary both in private and public prayer for believers to kneel when presenting their petitions. "O come, let us worship and bow down: let us kneel before the Lord our maker" (Ps 95.6).

If we do kneel to pray, it should be an indication of reverence and humility before the One Whom we petition. The attitude of our hearts is most important; it is easier to bow the knee than to bow the heart. We are approaching a "throne **of grace**" (Heb 4.16), but it is a throne nevertheless, and the One Who sits on the throne possesses regal majesty. It is fitting that His dignity should be respected, even although we come to Him as children to a Father. While we have "boldness to enter into the holiest by the blood of Jesus" (Heb 10.19), the same book of the Bible reminds us that we ought to religiously serve Him "with reverence and godly fear" (ch.12.28).

The bowed knee is one way by which our deference to Him can be expressed. Please allow a personal touch at this point. In addressing Him, I have tried to maintain a form of language that was the usual way of addressing God when I was young. It is a little different from the way I speak to others and may be regarded as somewhat archaic now, but my personal feeling is that our English language allows me opportunity to use a mode of expression that acknowledges the uniqueness of the One Whom I address. As stated, this is a personal conviction, but for me, it appropriately complements the bended knee.

Prostration

When He addressed His Father in the Garden of Gethsemane, the Lord Jesus was not merely on His knees, but "he fell on his face, and prayed" (Mt 26.39). Joshua was on his face because of shame and perplexity (Josh 7.6). The Samaritan leper was on his face in gratitude (Lk 17.16). But the Lord Jesus was on His face in deep agony of spirit as He looked onwards to the cross. In one of his hymns, Isaac Y. Ewan captured something of the intensity of the torment that He anticipated.

Garden of gloom appalling,
Where, in His sore amaze,
Earthward in anguish falling,
Prostrate, *the Saviour prays;*
Prays in exceeding sorrow,
Prays, on the ground bowed low
Facing the dark tomorrow
Full of unfathomed woe!

While you will never come anywhere near our Lord's experience in the Garden, it could be that there are times when you feel that circumstances are crushing you to the extent that you actually lie prone in the presence of God as He did, and express "A prayer of the afflicted, when he is overwhelmed, and poureth out his complaint before the Lord" (Heading of Psalm 102).

Standing

When two of Abraham's visitors left his encampment, "Abraham **stood** yet before the Lord. And Abraham drew near, and said … " (Gen 18.22-23). So Abraham was standing while he spoke to God, and God was "communing with Abraham" (v 33). At the time of the golden calf incident, "Moses … **stood** before him (God) in the breach" (Ps 106.23). Jeremiah spoke to God about the ingratitude of people for whom he had interceded; "I **stood** before thee to speak good for them" (Jer 18.20). These spiritual giants were content to stand patiently in the presence of God to make their appeals for the people. So it is not inappropriate to stand to pray. In prayer meetings in the western world, generally, brothers who participate stand when praying. In some cultures, the whole congregation stands for the prayers.

If we are practising the on-the-move style of praying without ceasing, living in the atmosphere of prayer, in any situation urgently and spontaneously speaking to God, we will be praying on occasions as we stand and as we walk!

Sitting

It was a morning of deep disappointment for David. The previous evening, without asking for God's guidance, the prophet Nathan had given him the go-ahead to build the temple of God (1 Chr 17.2). He had to return the next morning to reverse these instructions. However, Nathan brought a promise from God that would more than compensate for David's crushing disappointment at being denied the honour of building God's house. God made a covenant with David, promising him that would be the head of a dynasty that would eventually introduce the Messiah to the world.

On receiving such a promise, "David the king came and sat before the Lord" (v 16). Abraham standing before the Lord perhaps indicates his sense of urgency. David sitting before Him seems to denote his quiet contentment with the Lord's will. He settled himself to delight in the presence of God. Although he was sitting, the words of his prayer did not in any way reflect a casual attitude to God. We can enjoy experiences like this when we spend longer periods of communion in the Lord's presence. The bride in the Song of Solomon declared, "I **sat down** under his shadow with great delight" (Song 2.3). Zealously she **ran** after him in ch 1.4. Now she is content to sit in his presence and enjoy communion with him.

Places

We have been referring constantly to the need to live in the atmosphere of prayer, so that we can speak to God anywhere at any time. Having said that, when it comes to what we called our regular appointments with God, the Lord Jesus spoke of entering your own room, closing the door, and praying to your Father in secret (Mt 6.6). If your accommodation allows it, have a place where on a regular basis you can be alone, in quietness, to privately address the Father. We observed that Daniel had his upper room for his three-times-a-day encounters with God.

There are records in the Bible of prayers that arose to God from a great variety of places. The Lord Jesus prayed on a mountaintop, in a wilderness, in a garden and, indeed, on a cross. Peter prayed at the temple and on a roof. Paul prayed on the seashore, by a riverside and in various prisons. Perhaps the most unusual place from which prayer ascended to heaven was when Jonah prayed from the belly of the great fish, but even from such a location, the prayer was heard and answered! The important and obvious point is that no matter where you are, and in whatever circumstances you find yourself, it is always appropriate to pray.

Chapter 7

PURITY

Unhindered Prayer

We come now to consider the fact that God requires what could be called 'moral suitability' on the part of those who come to Him in prayer. Put more simply, there is the need for good behaviour. This is implied in a verse quoted right at the start: "The effectual fervent prayer of **a righteous man** availeth much" (Jas 5.16), with Elijah cited as an example of a righteous man. True, Elijah's prayer was believing prayer. When he prayed that it would not rain, he was basing his confidence on the fact that God had said that drought would be the inevitable outcome of idolatry, and the people had become very idolatrous. His prayer was also earnest prayer as verse 17 states. So it was a faith-filled, fervent prayer, but he also had the moral right to expect that God would respond to his prayer, because he was a righteous man – he personally had been behaving well in spite of the blatant rebellion of everyone around him.

So then, there is need for holy living if we really expect God to respond to our prayers. The psalmist put it this way, "If I regard iniquity in my heart, the Lord will not hear me" (Ps 66.18). Solomon agreed: "He that turneth away his ear from hearing the law, even his prayer shall be abomination" (Prov 28.9). Even the man who had been blind from his birth knew that: "We know that God heareth not sinners: but if any man be a worshipper of God, and doeth his will, him he heareth" (Jn 9.31). The principle is that if we are tolerating sin in our lives, we cannot expect God to respond to our prayers. Sin in the life could be one reason for unanswered prayer.

Those who participate in public prayer meetings must be equally qualified as far as their conduct is concerned. When speaking about an assembly prayer meeting, Paul said to Timothy, "I will therefore that men pray every where, lifting up **holy** hands, without wrath and doubting" (1 Tim 2.8). No one needs to be "gifted" to take part in a prayer meeting; what God is looking for are the holy hands, in other words, a life that is not besmirched by sin. "The prayer of the upright is his delight" (Prov 15.8).

Unanswered Prayer

As just noted, unjudged sin in our lives is a definite hindrance as far as the effectiveness of prayer is concerned. An illustration of this is in a verse that Peter specifically addressed to husbands. He spoke of the possibility of prayers being hindered if a husband does not treat his wife with respect (1 Pet 3.7). King Saul's persistent and varied bad behaviour placed him in a position in which God ignored his prayers: "When

Saul enquired of the Lord, the Lord answered him not" (1 Sam 28.6).

Unconfessed sin is not the only reason for what we call unanswered prayer. James indicates that in our prayers we could be asking for the wrong things. "Ye ask, and receive not, because ye ask amiss, that ye may consume it upon your lusts" (Jas 4.3). It could be that some of our prayers are rather selfish; we have our eye on something that could be to our advantage, and God kindly withholds it from us, simply because it would be an impediment to our spiritual progress. He knows what is best for us. It is when we ask "according to his will" that He hears us (1 Jn 5.14). There is a sad event in Israel's history when they were persistent in their demands for meat. There is a commentary on that incident in the Psalms: "He gave them their request; but sent leanness into their soul" (Ps 106.15). A statement like that should cause us to question our motives before we ask for something specifically, and it challenges us to assess accurately how we would be affected if the insistent request was granted. Would it rob me of time that I could otherwise use in the service of God? Would it betray a tendency to focus on the material rather than the spiritual? How would it impact the family? Would it interfere with my commitment to the assembly? To go back to the language of the Psalm, would it bring leanness of soul? These could be some of the considerations to take into account when we make a personal ambition a matter of earnest prayer.

Our prayers must be in line with the will of God. Those who

advocate the "name it and claim it" philosophy fly in the face of Bible teaching when they tell us to request our desire by faith without ever inserting the rider, "Thy will be done". Even the Apostle Paul, who had a greater insight into God's leading than we have ever had, was quick to acknowledge the need to adapt his plans to the will of God. For example, he had a great desire to visit Rome, and this is how he described his prayers for that. "Making request, if by any means now at length I might have a prosperous journey **by the will of God** to come unto you" (Rom 1.10). His ambition to visit the metropolis was from a pure motive, and yet he was aware of the need of God's superintending hand. It is true that James instructs us to "ask in faith, nothing wavering" (Jas 1.6), but as ever, context must be taken into account. James is speaking specifically about the need for wisdom in the face of persecution. If a believer feels at a loss to know how to handle a situation, he should "ask in faith" for the necessary know-how. Faith is not a blank cheque, a way of forcing God to give us what we want.

A delay in receiving an answer to a prayer may cause us to feel that God has not heard. It has often been said that God's delays are not necessarily God's denials. In other words, the fact that there is not an instant response does not mean that God will never respond to the request. This is illustrated in the lives of John the Baptist's parents, Zacharias and Elisabeth. They had no family, and obviously had been praying for a child. Life had slipped past and both of them were now elderly. However, Gabriel appeared to Zacharias as he ministered in the temple, and the angel's announcement was, "Thy prayer is heard" (Lk 1.5-13). The lesson is that we should be persistent if we are convinced that our prayer is not self-centred. It could be a delay rather than a denial. Never stop being burdened before God for a wayward family. The Lord's own brothers were unbelievers (Jn 7.5), but on the last occasion that they feature as a family in Scripture, they were at a prayer meeting (Acts 1.14). Never give up on anyone!

Everything God plans is far superior to anything that we could ever had anticipated; He "is able to do exceeding abundantly above all that we ask or think" (Eph 3.20). Thus there are denials that are actually for our spiritual good. Paul had what he called "a thorn in the flesh". Three times over he asked for it to be removed and God turned down that request. Reflecting on it, Paul could detect God's wisdom in allowing that trial to persist; it was all calculated to keep him humble. There was the danger that because of his unique privileges, including being caught up to the third heaven, pride could have crept into his heart. To keep him from becoming "exalted above measure", the thorn remained. However, there was this compensation, "My grace is sufficient for thee". While the trial was going to be permanent, the Lord would provide necessary grace, allowing him to cope. This grace helped him to understand that it was all in the divine plan for his spiritual good, and for his further effectiveness in service, for Christ's "strength is made perfect in weakness" (2 Cor 12.1-10). It is difficult for us to glory in infirmities as Paul did, and maybe like him we have pleaded earnestly for a trial to end. If there seems to be no end, it would be wonderful if we could be given necessary grace too, and see in the situation the pressure of the hand of the Potter as He moulds us into what He wants us to be. We might not see it all too clearly here and now, but like Mrs. Cousin we will be able to say;

> *I'll bless the hand that guided,*
> *I'll bless the heart that planned,*
> *When throned where glory dwelleth*
> *In Immanuel's land.*

So then, there are a number of reasons why our prayers may not be answered as we would have expected, and "No" is the answer! To quote a little poem that Amy Carmichael wrote as a child:

> *Jesus answered, He said, "No"*
> *Isn't "No" an answer?*

Chapter 8

THE PRAYER MEETING

Personal Observations!

"Pray without ceasing" (1 Thess 5.17). As noted earlier, it is a vital command, but it has no reference to extended prayers in the prayer meeting! This statement is not original, but I endorse it: "There are two things that spoil a prayer meeting, the first is the long pauses, and the other is the long prayers". I know that pauses can give time for reflection, but interminable silences give rise to wandering thoughts on the part of all but the most focussed. Equally, the long prayers in public prayer meetings tend to create a dull atmosphere.

There is no Scripture that prescribes either a minimum or maximum time frame for a public prayer, but the Lord Jesus raised a warning. He said of the Pharisees that "for a pretence" they made their long prayers (Mt 23.14 AV). The criticism was that their long prayers were a sham, part of the outward show of piety that they wanted to project. There is the danger that public prayers can lack the reality that we really need. Those who participate should constantly keep in mind the question, "Who is it that we are addressing?" Do we really need to explain the meaning of a passage of Scripture when speaking to God? When we tell God about a situation that grieves us is it really a complaint against another believer? Hypocritical praying is a shameful thing.

In some prayer meetings, prayer points are outlined at the start. **Not every brother has to pray for every point**. It is better for a brother to pray twice more briefly, than to occupy an extended time all at once. There are occasions when a particular burden or emergency does dominate a prayer meeting. When Peter was in prison with his execution scheduled for the next day, the believers gathered and "prayer was made without ceasing of the church unto God for him" (Acts 12.5). I would think that every participating brother prayed earnestly for Peter.

Priority

From the first days of the church, priority was given to public prayer meetings. So far, we have focussed on guidance to help in our personal devotions, but there can be occasions when in an emergency, a few believers can join together and earnestly supplicate God about a specific matter. This is what Daniel and his friends did when a crisis arose suddenly in his life (Dan 2.17-18). However, the purpose of these few paragraphs is to give guidance from Scripture regarding what we describe as the assembly prayer meeting.

It began on day one, when the converts of the Day of Pentecost among other things "continued stedfastly … in prayers" (Acts 2.42). Throughout the Acts, crisis conditions occasioned impromptu prayer meetings as when Peter and John were released from prison with the threats of the authorities ringing in their ears (ch 4.23-31). As already cited, when James was martyred and Peter was expected to go the same way in the morning, "prayer was made without ceasing of the church unto God for him" (ch 12.5). These incidents demonstrate that saints can be called together to pray about a situation outwith what would be regarded as the regular "prayer meeting night". However, it seems clear that the early church did have set times for prayer as did the Jews; for them, the ninth hour was "the hour of prayer" and it was then that Peter and John encountered the lame man at the Beautiful gate of the temple (Acts 3.1).

Paul gives teaching about the prayer meeting in 1 Timothy 2. 1 Timothy is all about behaviour in the house of God (ch 3.15) and a range of topics is covered, but the apostle gets to the core of his subject at the beginning of chapter 2. The "first of all" with which he commences the chapter indicates the priority of congregational prayer (1 Tim 2.1). It is sadly possible that what was of major importance to Paul has slipped down the list of priorities for many Christians today. There are some who would never miss the breaking of bread but are not consistent in their attendance at the prayer meeting. David Newell once described the prayer meeting as "the Cinderella of assembly gatherings". It is significant that God noted the names of those who attended the prayer meeting in Acts 1.13-14. I have a feeling that He still marks the register on the prayer meeting night! We should make it a priority to be there.

Prayers

It is in connection with the prayer meeting that Paul lists the different aspects of prayer that we considered earlier, "supplications, prayers, intercessions and giving of thanks" (1 Tim 2.1). With such variety, there is no need for the public prayers to be stereotyped or repetitive. The scope of the prayers is so wide, for "all men", including all in positions of authority (vv 1-2). Since one of the responsibilities of any government is to maintain law and order (Rom 13.3), if we pray for their success in that field it will contribute to us leading "a quiet and peaceable life in all godliness and honesty" (1 Tim 2.2). "All men" includes people whom we have never met and maybe never will, but if we hear of them we can pray for them. A situation in a remote place may be brought to our attention, and we may never know if there has been a positive answer to the prayers, but congregationally it can be brought to God's "throne of grace". Think of the privilege we have of speaking to God on behalf of our fellow men.

Participants

All believers are expected to be at the prayer meeting, men and women. We have referred already to the fact that the Spirit of God recorded the presence of the women in Acts 1.14. 1 Timothy 2.9 anticipates that the sisters will be there, dressed modestly and unostentatiously. As far as audible participation is concerned verse 8 indicates that only the men will take part. It has often been pointed out that the Greek word for "men" in verse 8 is a different word from verse 1 where we are encouraged to pray for "all men". There the word is the generic term meaning mankind, men and women. The word that is used in verse 8 is a word that means males. Thus Paul is indicating that only male voices will be heard. The general principle of 1 Corinthians 14.34 holds good for the prayer meeting as with every other assembly gathering, "Let your women keep silence in the churches: for it is not permitted unto them to speak". While only males participate publicly, we made clear earlier that the brothers who do lead the assembly in prayer must have "holy hands". Bad behaviour disqualifies.

While the Christian women do not pray audibly at the prayer meeting, they do pray! Prayers can be expressed silently as can worship. Most would probably agree that the greatest expression of worship in the New Testament was when Mary of Bethany anointed the Lord Jesus Christ (Jn 12.1-3). That worship was expressed silently from her heart; we do not know of her speaking a single word. As far as prayer is concerned, Hannah is the example of silent prayer: "she spake in her heart; only her lips moved, but her voice was not heard" (1 Sam 1.13). Thus at the prayer meeting, the sisters will be there with as much to pray about as the men, and as burdened as any man could be. Their prayers will be expressed inaudibly in their hearts, and the omniscient God will take them into account. He will respond as surely as if these prayers had been heard by the whole congregation. To go back to James Montgomery's hymn;

Prayer is the soul's sincere desire,
Uttered or Unexpressed,
The motion of a hidden fire
That trembles in the breast.

Let us all be like the converts of the Day of Pentecost then, and "continue stedfastly … in prayers" (Acts 2.42).

Chapter 9

PRACTICAL ADVICE

Most of what has gone before is a summary of the Bible's teaching about prayer. Now there is the challenge to put what we know into practice in the routine and busyness of daily living. There can be many hindrances to a structured effective prayer life, and this final chapter will address some of these.

Time

There are so many things to do in a day and we feel that there are insufficient hours to accomplish all our plans! If we are honest, we know that we are able to prioritise, and we generally find time for the things that we **really** want to do. Prayer is something that, apart from God, no one knows whether we have engaged in it or not. We do not have to report to anyone that we have prayed today. That is why it is so easy to relegate prayer and to allow other things to come before it in our list of priorities. We really need to be determined, devoted, and disciplined if this crucial part of our lives is not to be neglected. Prayer takes time and we must **make time** for it.

Memory

No doubt there are people for whom you pray on a daily basis because they are close to you and dear to you. We all know though, that it is impossible to pray every day for everyone that we know, or for every need with which we are acquainted. For this reason, it can be helpful to have a prayer list – a journal, a notebook, a card system – some way of bringing to mind individuals and matters for prayer. Divide your list into categories and topics. Some will require daily intercession; others remember systematically. Use the list only as a memory prompt and not as a checklist to be ticked off! Pray earnestly for each.

Paul had the believers in Philippi in his memory and in his heart as he prayed often for them (Phil 1.3-8). It would be good for us to remember every believer in the assembly with which we are connected. Do it daily if that is possible, but if the company is very large, still pray regularly for each individual. Doing this will help to maintain a sense of oneness, and will smooth over difficulties and irritations.

We have noted that the Lord's work and workers need our prayers. There are missionaries all over the world for whom you can pray. Some Christians use a world map as a visual aid to assist memory. Again, it could be difficult to include every field of service every day. It may be helpful to divide the world into segments and focus on a different area each day.

As you listen to a missionary report or a letter from

a missionary, note some of the items for which prayer is requested. The Holy Spirit may focus your mind on some of the particular needs, and these can be brought to the Throne in your prayer times. Then there are publications which highlight a different missionary for each day of the month, and these could be incorporated in your prayers as well.

Probably the best way for you to be involved is for you to be in contact with some of the Lord's servants yourself to ask about their work and specific items for which you can pray. A text, an e-mail, or even an old fashioned letter would be appreciated. You would know then that you are part of that work and your prayers are contributing to it.

Concentration

A problem that we all have is that of remaining focussed and undistracted when praying. External distractions must be dealt with. The Lord Jesus spoke of closing the door to shut out all other things. For us today, that would include silencing the phone and any other device which may signal for our attention.

Wandering thoughts and drowsiness have to be overcome too. In the Garden of Gethsemane Peter, James and John were under orders to "Pray that ye enter not into temptation". We know that when the Saviour returned they were sleeping, and Luke the doctor explains the cause, "sleeping for sorrow" (Lk 22.40-45), and sometimes weariness and heaviness of heart can affect us that way – we don't feel like praying. We have no right to criticise the three apostles; have *you* never become drowsy when praying? Has there never ever been a lapse of concentration? Have your thoughts never wandered? John Nelson Darby spoke for us all when he wrote the words:

> *O Lord, Thy love's unbounded!*
> *So sweet, so full, so free!*
> *My soul is all transported*
> *Whene'er I think of Thee.*
> *Yet, Lord, alas! what weakness*
> *Within myself I find;*
> *No infant's changing pleasure*
> *Is like my wandering mind.*

It really is a great mercy that there is One Who pities us like a father, One Who "knoweth our frame; he remembereth that we are dust" (Ps 103.13-14).

One suggestion for overcoming the concentration problem is to pray out loud. If your circumstances allow this it may be worth considering. Some find it helpful to read the Scriptures aloud too, another thing to consider!

Conclusion

After all that has gone before there is only one more thing to say on the subject of prayer – **DO IT – PRAY**.

Do it sincerely, earnestly, specifically, persistently, regularly, unselfishly, thankfully and believingly. "Continue in prayer, and watch in the same with thanksgiving" (Col 4.2). Have confidence in the God to Whom you come. He is omnipotent, faithful, caring and generous. "And this is the confidence that we have in him, that, if we ask any thing according to his will, he heareth us" (1 Jn 5.14).